BUGS IN THE BACKYARD

Kathy Bjornestad and Heidi Stefanich

Photography by Heidi Stefanich
Illustrations by Kaya Glasner

Beartown
Press

BUGS IN THE BACKYARD

DEDICATIONS

To my husband, who is first and always the scientist I turn to.
-Kathy

To my husband Matt, who is my assistant, consultant, and companion in photog-
raphy, science, and most importantly, love and life.
-Heidi

CONTENTS

BUG, INSECT, OR ARACHNID?

Bugs in the Backyard isn't just a book about bugs. We often call all creepy-crawlies "bugs," but really, bugs are a specific type of insect. True bugs have a straw-like mouth. They change into adults in only two stages (nymph to adult), instead of four stages like other insects. Most feed on juices, though a few do nibble on humans and animals. All bugs are insects, but not all insects are bugs.

Arachnids are an entirely different animal. Though we often call them "bugs," they are quite separate from insects. Instead of having a head, thorax, and abdomen, they have only a head and abdomen. They also lack wings and a larval stage. Miniature adults emerge from their eggs fully formed. Spiders have eight legs, not six as insects do. They also make silk, while insects do not. So even though *Bugs in the Backyard* isn't exactly an accurate title, it has a catchy ring to it, don't you think?

INSECT OR BUG?

A bug is an insect no matter which kind,
but insects aren't bugs very much of the time.
Simpler by half is a true bug's life phases.
From nymph to adult, he will morph in two stages.
His mouth (or proboscis) is also a clue.
He uses that straw-mouth to nibble on you!
Yes, bed bugs and stink bugs are well-named, though drab.
Just so, the old pill bug (who's more like a crab).
Cicadas and aphids sport fancier names,
but all are still bugs of the insect domain.
A bug is an insect, but insects are picky—
to have the name "bug" is a little bit tricky.

Scientists estimate that there are around 10 QUINTILLION insects living on earth at any given time. That's a 10 with 18 zeros behind it—10,000,000,000,000,000,000!!!

Insects bite...

and bugs suck!

FLIES, BEETLES, AND MANTISES

PRAYING MANTIS

He eats the aphids and the flies.
He'll even try a mouse.
His appetite cannot be stopped—
it's bigger than a house.
The farmer loves to see him show
his angled head each fall,
and chase mosquitos from the pond—
a full-on green assault!
No other insect looks like him,
with front legs bent in "prayer."
But fly, you moths, he's not a saint!
He'll snatch you from the air!
A frog or lizard isn't safe,
and hummingbirds should flee,
for when this mantis comes to town
he's on a killing spree!

Using its single ear located on the underside of its abdomen, a praying mantis can detect a bat's ultrasound transmissions. It can take a nosedive to avoid being caught and eaten. This maneuver is also used by military fighter pilots under pursuit.

HANGING THIEF ROBBER FLY

I dangle by my forelegs.
A leaf is my trapeze.
From there I feast on houseflies
and calmly munch on bees.
I'm great at mid-air grabbing.
I'm excellent at stabbing.
I hunt with super vision
and catch bugs with precision.
They call me thief and robber,
but hey, a guy must eat.
A wasp is super tasty . . .
and dragonfly's a treat!

Once the hanging thief robber fly (also called assassin fly) has snatched its prey from midair, it injects venomous saliva into its victim, killing it almost instantly and liquifying the prey's guts. These are sucked out by the assassin fly's long, straw-like mouthpart called a proboscis.

DOGBANE BEETLE

With iridescent shimmer,
on milkweed leaf he moves,
metallic beetle glimmer—
he rocks his insect groove.
With sequined shell a-winking
in sun of early June,
he flashes, brightly blinking
and shines beneath the moon.
Until I saw this cutie,
I thought all beetles bland,
but clothed in blue-green beauty,
he's made me quite a fan!

As the dogbane beetle munches on its host plant, dogbane, it stores poisonous chemicals from the plant in specialized glands. Later, if threatened by predators, the beetle can ooze this toxin to ward off an attack. Its bright colors give would-be predators fair warning of its nasty poison defense.

LADYBUG

She's not at all a lady,
more like a knight in armor
who flies in search of aphids,
assisting grateful farmers.
We love to see her sitting
on spinach leaves at rest
or perched on stalks of broccoli,
protecting them from pests.
She's seven-spotted lucky,
at least that's what they say,
but I just love to watch her—
red-winged—she flies away.

A single ladybug can eat over 5,000 insects in its lifetime, which can be as long as 2 to 3 years in the wild. Considering it spends about one year in the adult stage, that would be like you eating more than 13 sandwiches every day!

DRAGONFLY

A tiny helicopter,
painted shades of blue,
you skim across the water
and pause to sip the dew.
You dive to ambush midges,
then swerve to gather more.
I watch your aerial antics
while fishing from the shore.
Your mission's solitary—
a captain without crew.
Beware the swifts and swallows,
or they might eat up *YOU*!

Dragonflies breathe through holes in their abdomens.

BEE FLY

I'm superfly!
I dive and dip
and hover near a flower,
turn on a dime
and take a sip
from tulips in the bower.*
I mimic bees,
but I don't sting.
My talent's in my mouth part.
A long proboscis
lets me reach
the lilac's luscious heart.

*A bower is a shelter built in a garden, often made of tree boughs.

Before they emerge as the cute and fluffy adults we see in our gardens, bee fly larvae start off as little carnivores, munching on solitary bee eggs laid underground!

SPIDERS

ARACHNID

I can't believe I'm in this book!
I've got *eight* legs . . . just take a look!
My eggs hatch into spiderlings.
There is no ugly larva thing!
My body comes in parts of *two*.
A thorax? I leave that for you!
I make a web, my food to trap.
Bugs "stick" around. I take a nap.
My glistening net keeps fresh the snack.
A tasty fly I never lack.
On threads of silk, I dangle high.
I only wish that I could fly.
That is the single skill those bugs
possess that I would truly love.
But I'm more scary—tricky, too.
Take that, insects! Who needs you?

With six joints on each of their eight legs, spiders have 48 knees!

CATFACE SPIDER

Why, oh, why are you called "catface?"
"Feline" doesn't match your look.
Lacking velvet nose and whiskers,
you could star in horror books.
Kitties own their share of creepy—
Halloween cats take the prize—
yet they're sleek and softly graceful,
beauty that one can't despise.
You are–pardon–downright creepy,
though your bite is mild compared
to your cousin brown recluse's,
and you lack tarantula's hair.
Black-striped legs and graceful sway
on orb-shaped webs you decorate
and the way you catch a fly
I guess I should appreciate.
But it's hard to love a spider,
even with a name like yours.
Maybe if you tried to smile more . . .
and replaced your fangs with purrs?

Did you notice the spider in the photo is missing a leg? Spiders will sometimes detach a leg to escape a predator or to get rid of an injured appendage. Even if the leg does not grow back, most spiders will survive just fine with seven or even fewer legs.

WOLF SPIDER

I hunt, hunt, hunt on the ground
without, out, out any sound.
My furry, furry stripes
help me hide in the grass,
under rocks, in the leaves,
as unknowing feet pass.
And my many, many eyes
help me see in the night
as a cricket jumps past,
sharp and clear in my sight.
And my legs scurry, scurry
as I run from the day,
big and buff, speedy tough
as I pounce on my prey . . .
In the dark, all alone,
by the shed,
near your home,
in the cellar,
'neath your bed . . .
Good *ni-ight*!

Wolf spiders are named after wolves, not because they're covered with fur and have fangs, but because of the chase-and-ambush hunting style they use to catch their prey.

GARDEN SPIDER

This yellow garden spider
has many other names
like "golden," "writing," "steeler"—
(but not of football fame).
She's "zigzag" and she's "zipper,"
"McKinley" if you like.
She crouches in the carrots,
waits patiently to strike.
But do not fear her venom.
Her tastes run more to flies.
She brightens up tomatoes—
adds color to their vines.
Her orb's a webby wonder.
Her extra claw's the key
to weaving fancy patterns
and catching bumblebees.
She stands for growth abundant—
a jewel bright and gold—
more common than you'd think her,
but lucky to behold.

A garden spider will often dismantle its own web at night, roll it up, and eat it! They
do this to recycle the protein needed to make their silk.

POLLINATORS

BUMBLEBEE

Little pollinator,
it's really hard to hate her.
There's fire in her bum,
but—oh—that lovely hum!

Bumblebees are able to sting more than once, though they rarely sting at all. Honeybees, on the other hand, will die when they sting because their barbed stingers remain stuck in the skin of their victims and pull out the insides of the bee.

SNOWBERRY CLEARWING

I'm neither hummingbird nor bee
yet pollinate quite happily.
Snowberry is my favorite treat,
a fragrant flower I love to eat.
I flit about within its buds—
the cutest moth there ever was.

A day-flying insect in the sphinx moth family, the snowberry clearwing is also known as a bumblebee moth because of its "fluffy" appearance and coloring. It is also sometimes called a flying lobster moth, due to its unique shape and distinctive, fan-shaped tail.

CATERPILLAR

I've been labeled pest and thief,
creeping forth and gnawing leaves,
eating through a farmer's grove,
munching milkweed—treasure trove!
But I *need* to gorge on greens
to become a beauty queen!
So I eat and eat and EAT
till my belly feels replete.
Then I curl in safe cocoon,
changing as the waxing moon
swells and rounds to fullest white
on one summer's perfect night.
Then, *ta-da!* I'm clawing free,
looking not a bit like me!
Cloaked in fire, a sunset sky . . .
I'll burst forth . . . a butterfly!

A single caterpillar can have up to 4,000 muscles in its body (around 250 in its head alone) to help with its wave-like movement. Humans have about 650 muscles, which means caterpillars possess about 6 times as many muscles as we do!

SWALLOWTAIL

She loves a wildflower meadow,
a bit of salvia blue,
a nip of rosebud nectar,
a sip of black-eyed Sue.
She's common as a housefly
but makes a prettier sight—
a flitting dance on patterned wings,
sun-kissed with golden light.

The caterpillar of a swallowtail butterfly is brown and white, resembling bird poop.
This makes it look less appetizing to would-be predators.

MELISSA BLUE

From April to August she flies,
through sagebrush plain
and mountain pine
to dine on alfalfa
and sweet lupine.
A butterfly
to mimic sky—
a sapphire on the wing.

Melissa Blue caterpillars secrete a sugary substance which ants feed on. The ants, in turn, offer the caterpillars some protection from predators.

MONARCH BUTTERFLY

She's queen mother of them all.
A thousand miles in search of food,
she flies to find a milkweed patch
to feed her hungry larvae brood.
She rubs her legs, a dainty wash,
before she dips into some phlox,
but many flowers suit her tastes
from salvia to hollyhock.
Her highness favors shades of orange.
A favorite, black-laced dress she wears
when choosing partners for a waltz
and dancing through the perfumed air.
Less and less I see her here
and miss her as the years go by.
The world becomes a darker place
when fewer monarchs fill the sky.

Monarchs are the only species of butterfly that makes a two-way migration from colder northern climates to warmer winter habitat in California and Mexico. Flying 50-100 miles per day, some travel as far as 3,000 miles one way!

POLLINATOR'S FEAST

Snapdragons, parsnip, and Joe Pye weed
grow blossoms the bees and the butterflies need.
Milkweed, coneflower, and wild bergamot,
a bouquet of plants that should not be forgot.
Stonecrop and goldenrod, aster and yarrow,
fuchsia, tall hollyhocks, sunflowers yellow,
dahlia, daisy, and small dandelion,
from showy to pesky, they're good for the garden,
to draw in the insects that drink up the nectar—
let's cheer for the blossoms and pollen collectors!

Seventy-five percent of earth's flowering plants (including many, if not most, human food crops) require animal pollination to exist. Insects make up about 199,999 of the 200,000 animal pollinators. The remaining 1,000 species include bats, hummingbirds, and small mammals.

HOW TO MAKE A POLLINATOR GARDEN

1. Choose a sunny to partly sunny spot where flowers and host plants that attract butterflies will grow well. Plant all kinds of sun-loving flowers to provide nectar. Also, grow host plants for caterpillars to munch on. If you want monarch butterflies to visit, be sure to cultivate milkweed. It's good to have flowering bushes or trees in your butterfly garden, too. They give shelter to insects.

   Common annual flowers to plant (must be replanted every year):

   sweet alyssum, marigolds, petunias, heliotrope, lantana, verbena, zinnias, and sunflowers

   Common perennial flowers to plant (come back year after year):

   asters, asclepias, coneflowers, hollyhocks, dahlias, and black-eyed Susan

   Common host plants:

   parsley, dill, fennel, borage, and milkweed

   *Go to **https://www.pollinator.org/** to find out what plants grow best for the butterflies where you live.

2. Place some flat stones in your butterfly garden. Butterflies enjoy basking in the sun.

3. Set up a butterfly feeder. Put a shallow dish with a lip in an old plant hanger, or use a bird bath. Place rotten fruit in the feeder. Butterflies really love gooey, brown bananas.

4. Put a big saucer among your flowers. Fill it with wet sand and yard soil. Keep it damp. The butterflies will drink from this. They don't like deep sources of water.

AUTHOR'S NOTE

Insects are often the "building blocks" of habitats. Pollinators like honeybees and butterflies help plants reproduce. Without them, many species of flowers and trees would die off. Speaking of pollinators, if pollinating midges went extinct, we wouldn't have chocolate! Beetles are the janitors of our world, cleaning skeletons, getting rid of waste, and eating up weeds. Silkworms produce 80% of the planet's silk. We also get other products from the insect world such as beeswax, dyes, medicines, and don't forget honey. There would be less variety of foods without insects. Many cultures *eat* insects. It may sound gross to you, but a roasted cricket might make an African person's mouth water!

Ninety percent of life on earth comes in the form of insects. Around 900,000 species of insects have been identified, but millions more might exist. The ecosystems of Earth maintain a delicate balance. When we upset the balance by endangering or killing off species, ripples spread throughout all other parts of the ecosystem. What can you do to help? Climate change is the main culprit. It threatens all of us, so limit your carbon footprint. Conserve water, electricity, and gas. Plant flowers.

BIBLIOGRAPHY

Anderson, Maria. "Killer Insect Profile: The Assassin Fly." *Smithsonian Institution*, 30 Nov. 2015, www.si.edu/stories/killer-insect-profile-assassin-fly. Accessed 28 June 2023.

"Benefits of Insects to Humans." *Smithsonian Institution*, www.si.edu/spotlight/buginfo/benefits.

Boggs, Joe. "Dogbane Beetle: A 4th of July Treat!" *Bygl.osu.edu*, 6 July 2020, bygl.osu.edu/node/1638. Accessed 25 Feb. 2023.

Buchmann, Stephen. "Eastern Tiger Swallowtail." *Www.fs.usda.gov*, www.fs.usda.gov/wildflowers/pollinators/pollinator-of-the-month/TigerSwallowtail.shtml. Accessed 28 June 2023.

"Do Bumble Bees Sting and Can They Sting More than Once?" *BuzzAboutBees.net*, www.buzzaboutbees.net/do-bumble-bees-sting.html.

"Endangered Insects?" *After Bite Insectlopedia*, 5 Dec. 2016, insectlopedia.com/endangered-insects/. Accessed 27 Jan. 2023.

Hannemann, Emily. "6 Fascinating Dragonfly Facts You Should Know." *Birds and Blooms*, 18 July 2022, www.birdsandblooms.com/gardening/garden-bugs/dragonfly-facts/.

Howard, Jules. *Encyclopedia of Insects*. Beverly: Wide Eyed Editions, 2020.

Kingsley, Emmanuel. "10 Incredible Caterpillar Facts." *AZ Animals*, 12 July 2022, a-z-animals.com/blog/10-incredible-caterpillar-facts/?from=exit_intent. Accessed 25 Feb. 2023.

"Ladybug Facts and Photos." *Animals*, 1 Mar. 2014, kids.nationalgeographic.com/animals/invertebrates/facts/ladybug.

"Life Cycle." *Monarch Joint Venture*, monarchjointventure.org/monarchbiology/life-cycle#gallery. Accessed 5 July 2023.

McAlister, Erica. "Cute and Fluffy: Meet the Bee-Flies." *Discover Wildlife*, www.discoverwildlife.com/animal-facts/insects-invertebrates/bee-flies/.

"Melissa Blue (Includes Karner Blue) Plebejus Melissa (W.H. Edwards, 1873) | Butterflies and Moths of North America." *Www.butterfliesandmoths.org*, www.butterfliesandmoths.org/species/Plebejus-melissa#:~:text=Caterpillar%20Hosts%3A%20Lupine%20(Lupinus%20perennis. Accessed 5 July 2023.

"Melissa Blue - Montana Field Guide." *Fieldguide.mt.gov*, fieldguide.mt.gov/ speciesDetail.aspx?elcode=IILEPG5020. Accessed 5 July 2023.

Mitten, Mandy. "Wolf Spiders - Facts, Venom & Habitat Information." *Animal-corner.org*, 2004, animalcorner.org/animals/wolf-spider/. Accessed 25 Feb. 2023.

Pollination Fast Facts: Gardeners. www.pollinator.org/pollinator.org/assets/ generalFiles/Pollination-Fast-Facts-Gardeners-2019.pdf. Accessed 5 July 2023.

Reynolds, Dylan. "Clearing up Confusion around the Snowberry Clearwing." *Chesapeake Bay*, 1 June 2020, www.chesapeakebay.net/news/blog/clearing-up-confusion-around-the-snowberry-clearwing. Accessed 5 July 2023.

Romero, Nick. "How Many Legs Does a Spider Have? - Functions, Structure, Characteristics." *Animalwised.com*, 14 Dec. 2022, www.animalwised.com/how-many-legs-does-a-spider-have-4501.html. Accessed 28 June 2023.

Sather, Patrick. "10 Incredible Wolf Spider Facts." *AZ Animals*, 11 July 2022, a-z-animals.com/blog/10-incredible-wolf-spider-facts/.

Szalay, Jessie. "Wolf Spiders: Bites, Babies & Other Facts." *Livescience.com*, Live Science, 25 Dec. 2014, www.livescience.com/41467-wolf-spider.html.

Transform Your Yard into a Butterfly Haven with These Tips." *Country Living*, 3 Feb. 2022, www.countryliving.com/gardening/garden-ideas/a38916850/how-to-make-a-butterfly-garden/. Accessed 27 Jan. 2023.

Trivedi, Bijal. "Praying Mantis Uses Ultrasonic Hearing to Dodge Bats." *Animals*, 19 Nov. 2002, www.nationalgeographic.com/animals/article/praying-mantis-hearing-bats-animals.

U.S. FOREST SERVICE. "Monarch Butterfly Migration and Overwintering." *Www.fs.usda.gov*, www.fs.usda.gov/wildflowers/pollinators/Monarch_Butterfly/ migration/index.shtml. Accessed 1 Aug. 2023.

"What's the Difference: Bug vs. Insect." *Accelerator*, 16 Sept. 2022, www.reconnectwithnature.org/news-events/the-buzz/what-s-the-difference-bug-vs-insect/. Accessed 1 Apr. 2023.

World Wildlife Fund. "Monarch Butterfly | Species | WWF." *World Wildlife Fund*, 2013, www.worldwildlife.org/species/monarch-butterfly.

"Yellow Garden Spider | National Wildlife Federation." *National Wildlife Federation*, 2019, www.nwf.org/Educational-Resources/Wildlife-Guide/Invertebrates/ Yellow-Garden-Spider. Accessed 1 Aug. 2023.

ACKNOWLEDGEMENTS

To the ladies who stuck by me for book 2: a thoughtful, honest, and encouraging trio of critics extraordinaire—Michelle, Holly, and Jean.
-Kathy

To my mom, Kathy, my dad, Scott, and brothers Dylan and Trey, who have each in their own way inspired me to live a life of curiosity, exploration, and appreciation of the natural world.
-Heidi

And once again, a special, HUGE thanks to the very talented Kaya Glasner for the beautiful art she adds to our books.
-Kathy and Heidi

ABOUT THE AUTHORS AND ARTIST

Kathy Bjornestad is a retired K-12 school librarian and Language Arts teacher. She is a Wyoming Fellowship for Creative Fiction recipient and received an honorable mention for the Neltje Blanchan Award. She has published several essays in *Christian Science Monitor Weekly* and has placed pieces in statewide anthologies such as *Pasque Petals* and the Scurfpea Publishing's annual anthology.

Heidi Stefanich is an award-winning photographer, early literacy teacher, part-time biologist, and full-time nature geek living in the Black Hills of Wyoming. She is especially excited to contribute her photos and fun facts to this book to encourage a love of reading as well as a curiosity and awareness of nature. You may peruse her online gallery at HeidiStefanichPhotography.com.

Kaya Glasner is an artist based in southern Arizona. She is part of the Illustration, Design & Animation Program at the University of Arizona. Kaya specializes in murals, book illustration character animation. Her animation and set-building work have been shown twice at The Loft Cinema in Tucson. For more information, visit https://www.professionalscribblesbykaya.com, or contact professionalscribblesbykaya@gmail.com.